Cath Senker

THE GREAT NATURE HUNT

MINIBEASTS

W

FRANKLIN WATTS

Franklin Watts

Published in paperback in Gre[...]
by The Watts Publishing Grou[...]

Copyright © The Watts Publis[...]

Series editor: Sarah Peutrill
Series designer: Matt Lilly
Cover designer: Peter Scouldin[...]
Picture researcher: Kathy Loc[...]
Illustrations: Andy Elkerton

Dewey number: 595.7
ISBN 978 1 4451 4530 3

Printed in China

Franklin Watts
An imprint of
Hachette Children's Group
Part of The Watts Publishing Group
Carmelite House
50 Victoria Embankment
London EC4Y 0DZ

An Hachette UK Company

www.hachette.co.uk
www.franklinwatts.co.uk

FSC
www.fsc.org
MIX
Paper from
responsible sources
FSC® C104740

Picture credits: **Alamy**/PHOTOTAKE Inc: 7TR; **Dreamstime. com**/Ajith.a:10BR, Albert Komlos 12L, Alberto Perez Veiga 13g, Armando Frazao ContentsT, 17CR, Bright 11BL, Cosmin Manci 17TR, Domiciano Pablo Romero Franco 17BC, 24T, Eprom 11AC, Geotrac 17TL, Henriki 11TL, Ignatius Budi Prasetyo 5TC, Joseph Calev 14BL, Matteo Malavasi 10L, Mauro Rodrigues 14TR, Milosluz 5BL, Orionmystery 11TR, Panichunter 16T, Pavelzizka 13d, Sandyloxton 26, Sarah2 11CL, 13b, Tomatito26 11BR, Tomo Jesenicnik 5B, Valentina Razumova 5TL, Viktorfischer 16BL, Wabeno 19B, Yap Kee Chan 4; **Matt Lilly:** 9CL, C, CR; **Shutterstock.com**/ Aleksandar Grozdanovski 15C, Alex Staroseltsev Cover, Alfonso de Tomas 13c, Andrey_Kuzmin 15TR, Bildagentur Zoonar GmbH 21B, Brian Lasenby 28BR, Cardaf 13i, Christian Musat 7CR, David Lee 11CR, dragi52 20, Evgeny Smirnov 27BL, FCG 25a, Florian Andronache 26CR, fritz16 25c, Henrik Larsson 14TL, 28TR, irin-k 15CL, 15TC, 25CR, 28BCL, Jordan Lye 17TC, Jps 5CL, 21T, Katoosha 12R, Khomkrit Phonsai 25b, Kovalchuk Oleksandr 25TR, Lisa S. 8TR, MarkMirror 6TR, 13a, Matteo sani 25TL, Mattia ATH 26TL, Mikhail Olykainen 24L, Mirvav 27CL, Montypeter 11, MonumentalArt 8L, neko92vl 15BCR, Pakhnyuschy 24BR, pattara puttiwong 22B, Paul Reeves Photography 18T, 28CL, paulrommer 7BR, Photocrea 7L, PHOTOFUN 22T, Pichitchai Contents page B, 5TR, Radu Bercan 8BR, Randimal 13TR, Ratikova 18B, rodnikovay 25d, Sarah2 27BR, Schanz 13f, Scott Sanders 14C, Sergiy Bykhunenko 10TR, Shutova Elena 15BR, skynetphoto 25CL, Stephen Rees 9BL, Sumikophoto 13h,19T, Trofimov Denis 6BL, Vadim Petrakov 13e, vnlit Contents C, 15CR, xpixel 25BCR, Yevgeniy11 15TL

Every attempt has been made to clear copyright. Should there be any inadvertent omission please apply to the publisher for rectification.

[CA]N YOU FIND SIX BLACK  ANTS HIDDEN ON THE PAGES?

CLARA IS OUT LOOKING FOR MINIBEASTS. CAN YOU FIND HER?

There are lots more puzzles in this book. You can solve them by reading the text or by looking closely at the photos. The answers are on page 30.

Contents

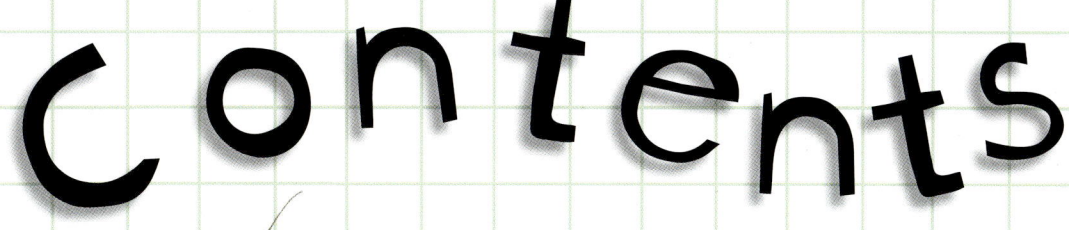

The great minibeast hunt

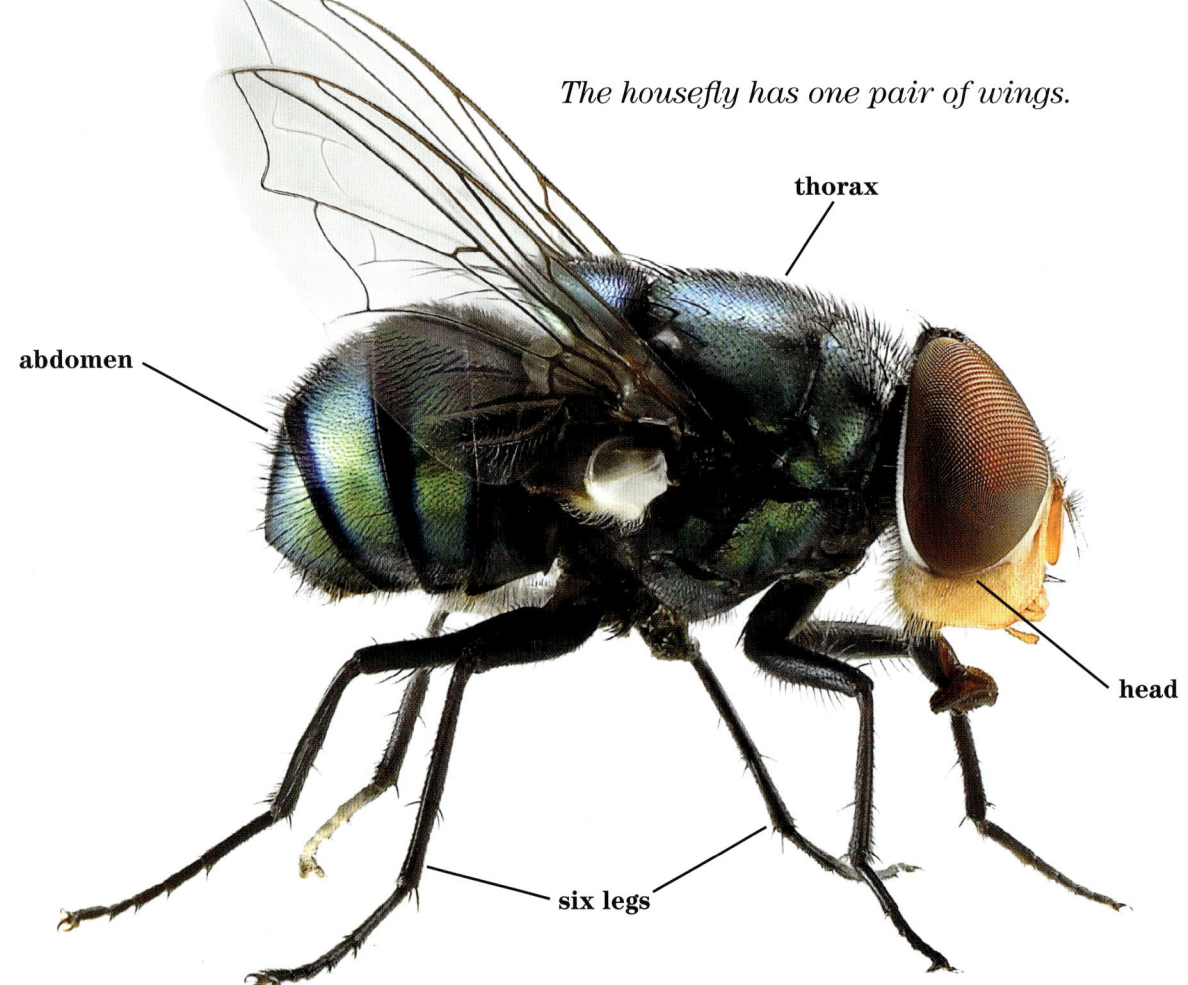

The housefly has one pair of wings.

thorax

abdomen

head

six legs

Minibeasts are insects, spiders and other small creatures. Worldwide, there are more than a million species of insect alone! Minibeasts are invertebrates – they have no backbone. Many are insects, with six legs and three body parts: a head, thorax and abdomen.

Most minibeasts have two antennae and two pairs of wings. Many kinds of minibeasts aren't insects though. Worms have no legs, spiders have eight legs, and and most millipedes have between 40 and 400 legs.

Minibeast homes

Minibeasts feed and shelter in various habitats. They are more active in spring, summer and autumn but you'll find some in winter too. You see them flying through the air, munching plants, hiding under rocks or buried in soil. They live in compost bins, water and even in our homes. So you can hunt for them right on your doorstep.

Am I an insect?

Which of these minibeasts are insects?

worm

ant

stick insect

bee

spider

millipede

THE MINIBEAST HUNT CHALLENGE

Bug hunting kit

Use a clean plastic tub with air holes in the lid, a small paintbrush for brushing minibeasts into the tub and a magnifying glass.

Flying minibeasts

In summer, watch out for minibeasts flying around garden flowers. Butterflies are active in the day. They usually have large wings in dramatic colours and patterns. Tiny scales on the wings turn light into vivid colours. The colours change depending on the angle from which you view them.

butterfly

Bumblebees and honeybees fly around, collecting nectar from plants. Listen for their humming sound – it comes from the movement of their wings. They are not aggressive (keen to fight) but they will sting you if they feel threatened. Some bees live alone but most live in colonies controlled by a queen bee. Wasps look similar to bees but are more likely to sting you, especially at the end of the summer.

bumblebee

Spot the difference

Butterfly wing patterns are symmetrical. Here we've altered the photos to create one difference between each wing. Can you spot them all?

Silver-spotted skipper

Red admiral

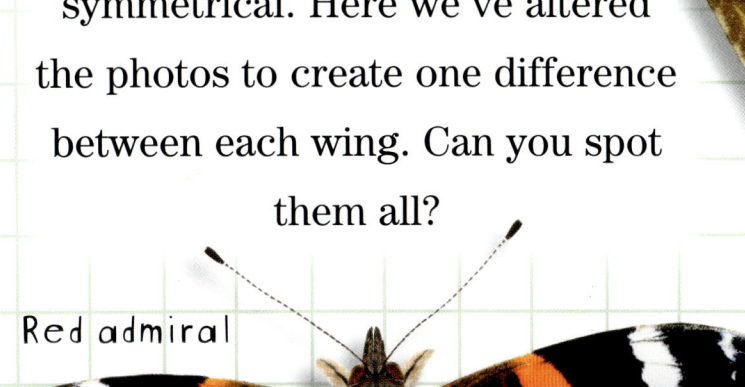

Cabbage white

THE MINIBEAST HUNT CHALLENGE

Butterfly feeder

Make four holes around the rim of a paper plate. Tie a 30 cm length of string through each hole. Tie the strings together. Add ripe fruit and hang near flowers.

Painted lady

On plants

Check under plant leaves in any season except winter – are slugs, snails or aphids lurking there?

snail

slugs

Slugs and snails both love to munch juicy leaves, but slugs are less fussy; they eat dead animals and plants too. With no legs, slugs and snails glide on one foot. You'll know if they're around because they leave a slimy trail. They move slowly but are excellent climbers. Slugs and snails like damp weather.

Aphids are tiny insects, including greenfly, blackfly and whitefly – you'll recognise them by their colour. They make holes in the stem of a plant and feed on the sap that comes out.

aphids

Minibeast maze

Use your fingertip to trace the right path so that each minibeast can reach its dinner.

snail

aphid

slug

a

b
lettuce

c

sunflower leaf

bean leaf

Minibeast meals

Gardeners hate snails, slugs and aphids because they damage plants, but these minibeasts are vital food for beetles, frogs and birds.

In the soil

Grab a trowel and dig around carefully in the soil. Except in midwinter, you'll probably unearth minibeasts such as worms and ants.

ant

Ants are insects with long antennae and powerful jaws. Their digging helps to improve the soil, and they feed on flies and other pests.

worms

Worms play a vital role in creating healthy soil for growing plants. They burrow down, making tunnels that let in air and water, and make space for plant roots to thrive. They bring down organic matter from the surface, such as leaves and grass, and mix it with the soil below to make rich plant food. When worms eat, they leave behind worm casts, which fertilise the soil.

Ant parts

Which of these body parts belong to an ant?

eyes

thorax

wings

jaws

shell

head

abdomen

antennae

On water

To hunt minibeasts near water, visit a pond or lake in spring, summer or autumn.

dragonfly

Look for brightly coloured dragonflies and damselflies flying rapidly over the pond. They look similar but, at rest, you can tell them apart. Dragonflies hold their wings out, while damselflies hug them to their body.

On the surface

Examine the surface of the water. Pond skaters are insects that move at great speed across the water on their legs, seizing dead and dying insects from the surface as they travel.

pond skater

Backswimmers and lesser water boatmen are both insects that swim and look similar, but the backswimmer swims upside down. Lesser water boatmen are vegetarians, eating algae, while the backswimmer feeds on insects and other tiny animals.

backswimmer

pond animals

Which of these minibeasts are found in ponds or flying over them?

a butterfly

b ant

c slug

d lesser water boatman

e pond skater

f worm

g damselfly

h bee

i snail

13

Hiding under rocks

woodlouse

In a park or garden, lift some rocks. Are any minibeasts sheltering there? Look carefully for woodlice, centipedes and millipedes. Woodlice are crustaceans that feed on rotting leaves and plants. If you touch a woodlouse, it will curl into a ball to protect itself. Many animals eat woodlice, including centipedes.

Centipedes and millipedes have many legs. How can you tell them apart? Centipedes have one pair of legs per segment. Millipedes have two pairs of legs on each segment.

millipede

segment

Centipedes are fast-moving hunters with a set of claws to grab and poison insects and other prey. Watch out – they can 'bite' you too. Millipedes are gentler creatures that eat rotting plants.

centipede

Find my habitat

Which habitat does
each minibeast prefer?

worm

bee

soil

moist leaves

dragonfly

snail

by water

THE MINIBEAST HUNT CHALLENGE

Which shelter?

Peg bits of cloth, clear
plastic and cardboard to the
ground. After a week, peek
underneath. Which shelters
the most minibeasts?

flowering
plants

In our homes

When it's cold, many minibeasts head for a warm shelter – sometimes in our homes. With a torch, look for spiders or crane flies lurking under furniture or in other dark places. Some ladybirds, moths and butterflies come indoors too. Try not to disturb them. If you prefer not to share your home with minibeasts, try to move them to a cool, protected place.

spider

Summertime

In summer, when people throw open the windows, flies and fruit flies often zoom into the kitchen. Indoors, they're pests, feeding on our food and spreading germs – keep food covered so they're less tempted to visit. Silverfish are also pests. Normally living indoors, these small, wingless insects munch starchy materials such as wallpaper and book bindings and can cause a lot of damage.

a fly feeding on ice cream

Odd one out

Which minibeast
is the odd one out,
and why?

fly

flea

spider

silverfish

crane fly

On your pet

If you have a cat or dog, it may get fleas,
which make it itch. Cat fleas can jump up
to 34 cm and keep jumping for
several days without rest!

Minibeast pollinators

Did you know that minibeasts keep us alive? Some flying minibeasts pollinate the flowers of fruit, vegetables and crops. The flowers then make seeds, which grow into new plants.

About one-third of the food we eat depends on pollination by animals. Bees are the most important pollinators, so they are vital to our world. Other insect pollinators include butterflies, moths and hoverflies.

a butterfly pollinates a flower

a bee sucks up nectar

Watch pollination

In spring and summer you can see pollination for yourself. Watch a bee collecting nectar from a flower. As it feeds, some of the pollen sticks to the hairs on its body but it also collects some pollen to feed to its young. It visits another flower of the same type and some of the pollen on its body rubs off. Now the flower can make seeds.

a bee collecting nectar.

Label the bee

Match the labels to the honeybee picture.

pollen basket   head

abdomen

wing   leg

eye

antenna

tongue

thorax

a

i

b

c

d

e

h

g

f

Minibeast pest controllers

A healthy park or garden teems with helpful minibeasts controlling pests. See if you can spot them at work.

This spider has caught a fly and a wasp in its web.

Spiders eat flies and other minibeasts that carry diseases. They build a web of strong, sticky silk, which traps insects that fly into it. The spider wraps its victim in silk and injects it with venom (poison), which turns its insides to liquid for the spider to suck out. Late summer and autumn are good times to watch spiders in their webs.

Find the fly

Use your finger to trace a path for the spider through broken strands of web so that it can reach the fly.

Ladybirds and beetles

This ladybird has caught an aphid.

On the ground, check for beetles. They make a meal of slugs and caterpillars, stopping these greedy feeders from damaging plants. Ladybirds are a kind of beetle. Look for them on bushes, branches, flowers and plants. They help gardeners by eating aphids such as greenfly. Count a ladybird's spots – no ladybird has more than 22.

Minibeast cleaners

Minibeasts such as beetles and hoverflies have an important job to do – they're nature's little cleaners. Along with fungi, they help to return dead materials to the soil. You'll find them in garden beds and compost heaps.

hoverfly

metallic wood-boring beetle

Beetles love rotting wood in particular. They bore holes in it. These often become nests for other minibeasts, such as solitary wasps and bees that don't live in colonies (see page 24). You can make a mini wood habitat to attract beetles and other minibeasts. Place a log at the back of a garden in a partly shaded patch that gets some sun. Minibeasts will enjoy the mixture of warmth and moisture.

Spot the minibeasts

How many beetles can you find in this garden? Which other minibeasts can you spot?

THE MINIBEAST HUNT CHALLENGE

Night hunt

Stand by an outside light on a warm, moonless evening. The light should attract moths and you'll be able to see beetles and spiders hunting for food.

Building nests

Some minibeasts are social – thousands live together in nests to protect themselves from predators. Watch out for these nests when you're walking in the countryside, but make sure you don't disturb them.

Honeybee nests are called hives. At the core is the honeycomb, made of six-sided wax cells. The queen bee lays her eggs here.

ants' nest

flying ant

Ants live in very organised and elaborate colonies, with long tunnels running underground. To make their nest, ants can lift materials 20 times their weight – if you could do that, you could lift a car!

24

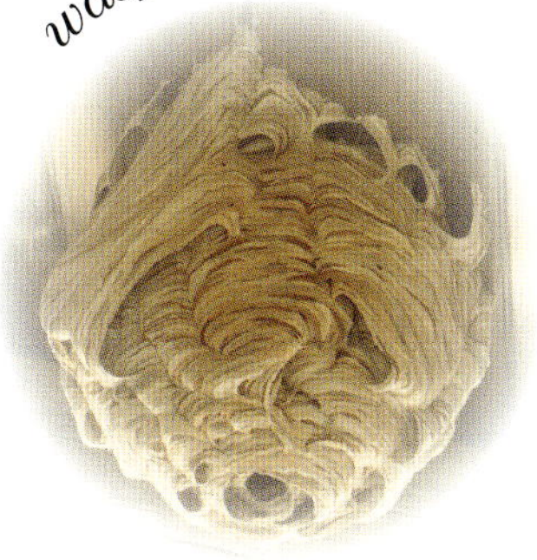

Wasps' nests

wasps' nest

wasp

Wasps build their nests using paste made by chewing dead wood and spitting it out. It dries to form paper-like walls. As more wasps are born, the worker wasps extend the nest.

STAY AWAY FROM WASPS' NESTS!

Which minibeast?

Match the minibeast to the nest. Only part of the nest is shown!

termite

wasp

bee

ant

THE MINIBEAST HUNT CHALLENGE

Bumblebee nest

Fill a large flowerpot with dry grass. Dig a hole under a bush. Half bury the pot at an angle so the pot bottom sticks out.

a

b

c

d

Minibeast life cycles

Minibeasts often change completely as they go through their life cycle. Butterflies lay eggs, which hatch into wriggly caterpillars. They grow fast, moulting (shedding their skin) regularly. When a caterpillar is fully grown, it turns into a pupa. Inside, its body changes into an elegant butterfly. It comes out of the pupa and unfurls its beautiful wings.

Other minibeasts lay eggs that hatch into mini versions of their parents, called nymphs. The grasshopper lays up to 150 eggs in a row and sprays them with a sticky substance to form a pod. The eggs hatch into nymphs. They feed hungrily on soft plants and grow rapidly, shedding their skin many times until they reach adult size.

tiny grasshopper nymph

Butterfly life cycle

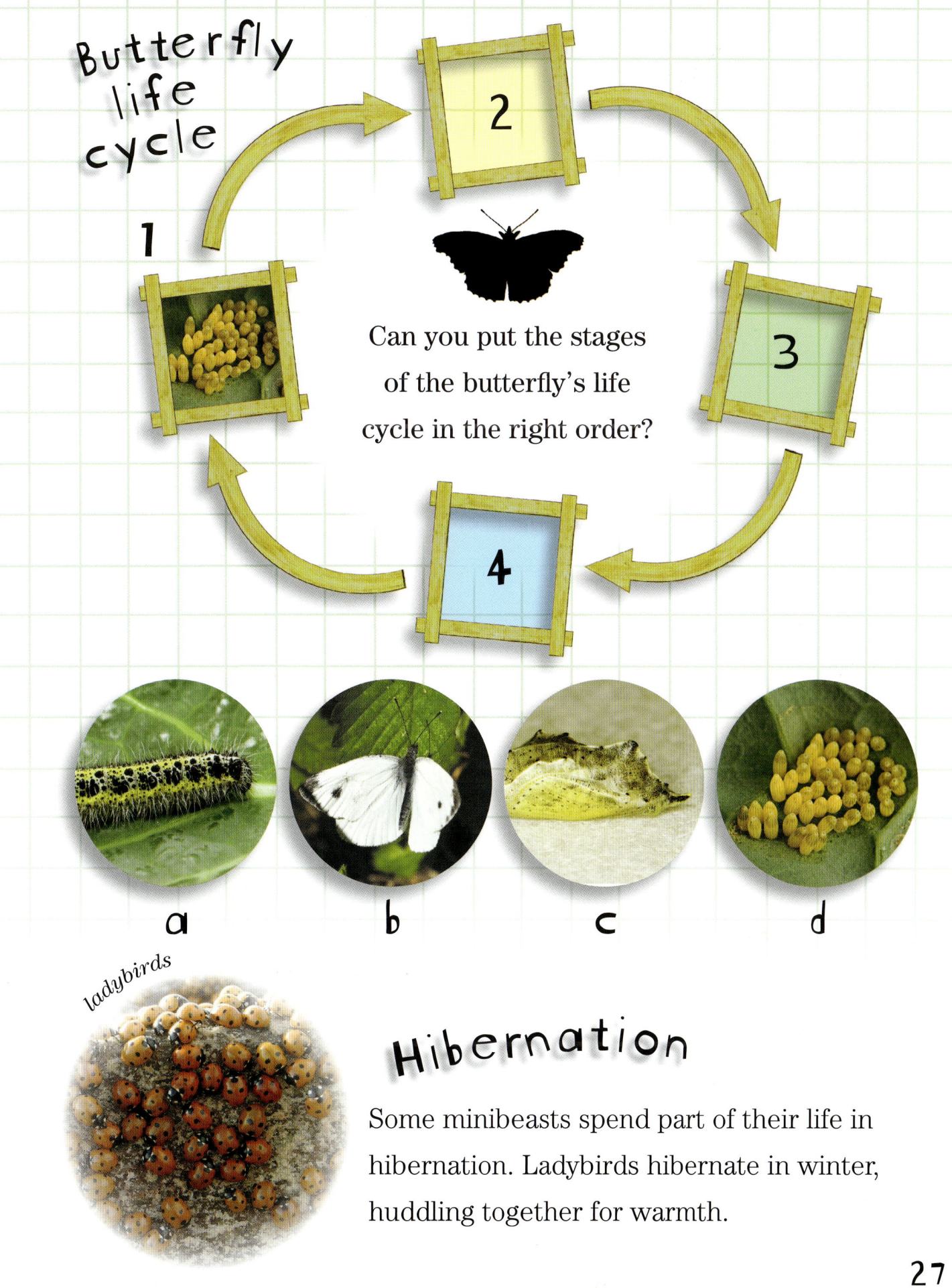

1

2

3

4

Can you put the stages of the butterfly's life cycle in the right order?

a

b

c

d

ladybirds

Hibernation

Some minibeasts spend part of their life in hibernation. Ladybirds hibernate in winter, huddling together for warmth.

Colour and camouflage

Minibeasts may be small but they're often bright and easy to spot. The vivid patterned wings of butterflies help them to attract a mate. They warn off predators too. The colourful markings mean 'I have a nasty taste'. Some butterflies, such as the monarch, are poisonous to other animals.

peppered moth

Other minibeasts use camouflage. They are the same colour as their habitat so predators and prey cannot spot them easily. The peppered moth has wing patterns that camouflage it against tree bark. Caterpillars and grasshoppers are green, just like the plants they feed on, and stick insects really do look like sticks.

monarch butterfly

Ladybirds are bright red. Some birds have learnt that this colour means the animal will smell and taste horrible, so they leave ladybirds alone.

stick insect

Minibeasts camouflage

Can you find the four camouflaged minibeasts in this picture?

THE MINIBEAST HUNT CHALLENGE

Make a minibeast-friendly garden
....
Grow wildflowers in flower beds or containers to attract bees and butterflies.

Puzzle answers

5 Am I an insect?
Ants, bees and stick insects are all insects.

7 Spot the difference
red admiral – should only have one red bar on the right wing
silver-spotted skipper – silver bar on the right wing is too short
cabbage white – brown spot missing from the left wing
painted lady – brown spot missing from right wing

9 Minibeast maze
a – aphid
b – slug
c – snail

11 Ant parts
The eyes, jaws, thorax, abdomen, head and antennae all belong to an ant.

13 Pond animals
d, e, g

15 Find my habitat
worm – soil
bee – flowering plants
dragonfly – by water
snail – moist leaves

17 Odd one out
The spider is the odd one out as all the others are insects.

19 Label the bee
a – wing
b – thorax
c – head
d – eye
e – antenna
f – tongue
g – leg
h – pollen basket
i – abdomen

21 Find the fly

23 Spot the beetles
5 beetles – other minibeasts: woodlouse, centipede and fly

25 Which minibeast?
termite – c
wasp – a
bee – b
ant – d

27 Butterfly life cycle
1 – d
2 – a
3 – c
4 – b

29 Minibeasts camouflage
caterpillar on leaf
moth on tree trunk
stick insect on branch
grasshopper on fallen leaf

Glossary

antenna (plural: antennae or antennas) One of the two long, thin parts on the heads of some insects (and some animals that live in shells), used for feeling and touching things.

aphid A very small insect that is harmful to plants. There are several types of aphid, including greenflies.

camouflage The way in which an animal's colour or shape matches its surroundings and makes it difficult to see.

cast A worm cast is the soil that has passed through a worm's body and is left in a small heap.

colony A group of plants or animals that live together or grow in the same place.

compost A mixture of rotted plants or food that can be added to soil to help plants grow.

crustacean An animal with a hard shell.

fertilise To add a substance to soil to make plants grow better.

fungi (singular: fungus) A living thing that is similar to a plant but without leaves, flowers or green colouring, and that usually grows on plants or on rotting things.

habitat The place where a particular type of animal or plant is normally found.

hibernate Of animals: to spend the winter in a very deep sleep.

nectar A sweet liquid that is produced by flowers. Insects such as butterflies and moths feed on it, and bees collect it to make honey.

organic Produced by or from living things.

pest An insect or animal that destroys plants.

pollen Fine powder, usually yellow, that is formed in flowers and carried to other flowers of the same kind by the wind or by insects, to make those flowers produce seeds.

pollinate To put pollen into a flower or plant so that it produces seeds.

predator An animal that kills and eats other animals.

prey An animal that is hunted, killed and eaten by another.

sap The liquid in a plant or tree that carries food to all its parts.

solitary Of an animal: one that does not live in a colony – for example, some types of wasp are solitary.

symmetrical Having two halves, parts or sides that are the same in pattern, size and shape.

Index

Websites

www.nationalgeographic.com/animals/invertebrates/
Find out more about bugs.

https://ypte.org.uk/factsheets/minibeasts/what-is-a-minibeast
Fact sheets about different minibeasts.

www.bbc.com/bitesize/clips/z44g9j6
A video about how minibeasts feed and defend themselves.

www.woodlandtrust.org.uk/naturedetectives/activities/
Activities about minibeasts and other wildlife.

*

Note to parents and teachers:
Every effort has been made by the Publishers to ensure that these websites are suitable for children, that they are of the highest educational value, and that they contain no inappropriate or offensive material. However, because of the nature of the Internet, it is impossible to guarantee that the contents of these sites will not be altered. We strongly advise that Internet access is supervised by a responsible adult.